FIRST-PERSON STORIES OF
WORLD WAR II BATTLES

BY NICOLE HOR

ROSEN PUBLISHING PRIMARY SOURCE LIBRARY

ROSEN PUBLISHING

Published in 2027 by The Rosen Publishing Group, Inc.
2544 Clinton Street, Buffalo, NY 14224

Designer: Deanna Lepovich
Editor: Nicole Horning

Cataloging-in-Publication Data

Names: Horning, Nicole.
Title: First-person stories of World War II battles / Nicole Horning.
Description: Buffalo, NY : Rosen Publishing, 2027. | Series: The Rosen Publishing primary source library | Includes glossary and index.
Identifiers: ISBN 9781725343047 (pbk.) | ISBN 9781725343054 (library bound) | ISBN 9781725343061 (ebook)
Subjects: LCSH: World War, 1939-1945–Juvenile literature. | World War, 1939-1945–Campaigns–Juvenile literature.
Classification: LCC D743.7 H67 2027 | DDC 940.54–dc23

Some of the images in this book illustrate individuals who are models. The depictions do not imply actual situations or events.

Manufactured in the United States of America

CPSIA Compliance Information: Batch #CSRYA27. For further information, contact Rosen Publishing at 1-800-237-9932.

CONTENTS

FOREWORD

History is so much more than just a boring collection of names and dates. It is a collection of stories—sometimes tragic stories, sometimes heroic stories, sometimes romantic stories, sometimes scary stories. And they're all stories of real people who lived real lives.

Those stories can get lost in the shuffle of memorizing battles, studying maps, and listing important court cases or rulers. That's why primary sources are so valuable. They remind us that historical events happened to and because of real people. Reading diaries, looking at photographs, and seeing newspaper articles are just some ways to make history feel personal through primary sources.

Another way is through watching or listening to interviews with people who lived through major historical events. That's what you're invited to do in this book—and all the books that are part of *The Rosen Publishing Primary Source Library*. Each chapter includes quotes from an interview with a real person who experienced a major historical event in a deeply personal way. You can also scan the QR code included at the beginning of each chapter to watch a video interview with the person featured in that chapter.

Created in partnership with Generations Broadcasting, *The Rosen Publishing Primary Source Library* was created to remind readers that there is power in sharing our stories. First-person stories make history come alive. And when history comes alive, we're better able to learn from it—and avoid the mistakes of the past.

The events you're living through today will be part of the next generation's history lessons. As you read and watch the stories collected here, think about what you want your story to be.

Note: More interviews about the topics featured in this series, as well as many other historical events, can be accessed v ia a subscription to Rosen Publishing's GBC Stories Database: rosendigital.com/GBCStories/.

HOW TO WATCH THE INTERVIEWS FEATURED IN THIS BOOK

- Use your phone's camera, and hold it over the QR code.
- Click the link that appears.
- Watch the video that pops up. If you would like to read a transcript of the interview while you watch, you can click on that option next to the video screen.

INTRODUCTION

World War II was one of the largest and most devastating conflicts in human history, lasting from 1939 to 1945. It involved countries across the globe and reshaped nations, economies, and societies forever. At its core, the war was fought between two major groups: the Axis Powers and the Allied Powers. The Axis included Germany, Italy, and Japan, nations led by leaders determined to expand their territories and influence through military conquest. The Allied Powers, on the other hand, included the United States, the United Kingdom, the Soviet Union, and China.

The war began in Europe on September 1, 1939, when Germany, under the leadership of Adolf Hitler, invaded Poland. This led to Britain and France declaring war on Germany, therefore starting the war. Over the next few years, Germany conquered much of Europe, including France, while Italy joined in support of the Axis powers. Meanwhile, Japan expanded across Asia and the Pacific.

Although the war was going on from 1939, the US initially stayed out of direct combat. Many Americans thought the US should stay out of what they saw as Europe's war, and Congress passed laws to limit US engagement. However, all of this changed on December 7, 1941, with the surprise attack on Pearl Harbor in Hawai'i. More than 2,400 Americans were killed, and nearly 20 ships were damaged or destroyed. The next day, the United States declared war on Japan, officially joining the conflict. Shortly afterward, Germany and Italy declared war on the United States, fully drawing the nation into the global struggle.

The United States' entry into the war dramatically shifted the balance of power. American soldiers, sailors, and airmen joined Allied forces fighting across Europe, North Africa, and the Pacific. Factories across the country worked around the clock to produce weapons, vehicles, and supplies, while citizens participated in rationing, war bonds, and other support efforts at home. The war would last nearly four more years after America joined, with battles that tested the courage and endurance of millions of service members.

World War II was marked by some of history's most intense battles, such as the Battle of the Bulge, as well as profound hatred and

After the surprise attack on Pearl Harbor that destroyed several battleships, the United States joined World War II.

human suffering. Six million Jewish people and millions of others lost their lives in the Holocaust carried out by Adolf Hitler and the Nazis.

World War II was also the first war in which nuclear weapons were used. In August 1945, shortly before the end of the war, the US dropped bombs on Hiroshima and Nagasaki, resulting in the total destruction of the cities, the loss of hundreds of thousands of lives, and long-term health effects such as cancer, leukemia, and reproductive issues in survivors.

World War II tested people and nations like never before, revealing the extremes of human cruelty as well as the heroism of soldiers on the frontlines. By the time the war ended in 1945, millions of lives had been lost, and the world had drastically changed politically.

CHAPTER ONE

BATTLE IN THE SKIES

During World War II, the fight against the Axis powers took place on the ground and in skies. Many soldiers flew dangerous bombing missions over enemy territory, targeting factories that contributed to the war effort. These missions were some of the most dangerous in the military, and resulted in heavy losses for many units, especially the "Bloody 100." In an interview, John "Lucky" Luckadoo, one of the most famous members of the Bloody 100, described his experiences in World War II.

THE BLOODY 100

New military service members were often quickly sent into dangerous combat during World War II. Some of these military units ended up being very famous and had a lot of losses during the war. John was assigned to one of these units, the Bloody 100, shortly after flying school:

Graduating from flying school, I was immediately assigned to a B17 outfit in Kearney, Nebraska, the 100th bomb group. It came to be known as the Bloody

Scan this QR code to watch John talk about being a member of the Bloody 100th flying unit, which suffered notoriously high losses of life.

John "Lucky" Luckadoo is one of the most famous members of the Bloody 100.

> *100th. I started flying combat in June of '43. If we completed or lived through 25 missions, we were rotated back to the states. Our chances of doing that were about one in four. Our initial losses were much greater than that. We had a 400 percent turnover in flying personnel in the first 90 days, so we became known as the Bloody 100th.*

The 100th bomb group was part of the US Army Air Forces' Eighth Air Force, which operated out of bases in England. From there, the bombers flew into Nazi-occupied Europe, targeting aircraft factories, oil refineries, and other key parts of Germany's war operations. The goal of targeting these operations was to weaken Germany's ability to produce weapons and supplies. By destroying these, the Allies hoped to slow down the German war effort and make it harder for them to continue fighting.

However, flying these missions was extremely dangerous. Bombers flew for hours at very high altitudes of about 25,000 feet (7,620 m), where there was little oxygen and temperatures were freezing, often at –40 (–40 degrees Celsius) or –50 degrees Fahrenheit (–45 degrees Celsius). Soldiers had to wear heavy gear and oxygen masks to fly the bombers while operating difficult equipment. Flying in tight bomber formations at such high altitudes with little oxygen was physically exhausting for the soldiers. Many gunners would also end up with frozen hands while firing at the enemy.

These missions were even more complicated by the enemy. German aircraft guns, which were called flak, would shoot at the planes. In addition to this, German fighter planes attacked the bomber formations to try to shoot them down before they reached their target.

The Purple Heart is given to service members killed or wounded in combat.

FAST FACT

THE PURPLE HEART IS AWARDED TO US SERVICE MEMBERS WHO HAVE BEEN WOUNDED OR KILLED IN COMBAT. IT WAS ORIGINALLY CREATED IN 1782 BY PRESIDENT GEORGE WASHINGTON AS A BADGE OF MILITARY MERIT THEN REDESIGNED IN 1932 TO RECOGNIZE THE SACRIFICE OF THE SERVICE MEMBER.

THE B-17 FLYING FORTRESS

The Bloody 100 used a heavy bomber called the B-17 Flying Fortress. This plane earned its nickname because it carried a lot of machine guns and was designed to defend itself against enemy fighters. B-17s often had 13 machine guns in different parts of the plane. Gunners were also positioned throughout the plane, allowing them to fire at enemy aircraft from nearly any direction.

Each bomber could carry 10 soldiers, and each position was important to the mission. The pilot and co-pilot flew the aircraft, the navigator guided the plane through enemy territory, and the bombardier aimed and released bombs at the target.

Other crew members helped defend the aircraft. Waist gunners fired from the sides of the plane while the tail gunner protected from attacks from behind. One of the most dangerous positions was the ball turret gunner, who sat inside a small rotating gun turret under the plane.

B-17 fighters flew in tight formations so that their guns could protect one another. When dozens of the aircraft flew together, the firepower made it more difficult for enemy fighters to approach. However, even with all of these defenses, the bomber crews still experienced heavy losses. Long missions over enemy territory tested the physical limitations, courage, and teamwork of every crew member on the B-17s.

A B-17 Flying Fortress is shown here at an air show in 2022.

FAST FACT

A STANDARD, HORIZONTAL, DIRECTION-REPORTING SYSTEM USES CLOCK POSITIONS. AN 11 O'CLOCK POSITION MEANS THE TARGET IS SLIGHTLY TO THE LEFT OF THE AIRCRAFT'S NOSE WHILE 9 O'CLOCK IS DIRECTLY TO THE LEFT, 3 O'CLOCK IS DIRECTLY TO THE RIGHT, AND 6 O'CLOCK IS DIRECTLY BEHIND.

DEADLY MISSIONS

During World War II, many military members were young men not long out of high school, flying into some of the most dangerous battles of the war. John described being young and in the Purple Heart Corner, which was the most vulnerable part of the formation. This is because this area of the formation was always heavily attacked by the Germans:

A destroyed hangar at the Messerschmitt factory is shown here.

Messerschmitt made powerful planes such as this one.

We were young kids. We were 19, 20, 21 years old. With the losses that we sustained, it was pretty hard to psych yourself up every day to get back in that airplane and go out and stick your neck out again...There was one particular mission, leading the low element of the three airplanes in the low squadron of the low group, which we call the Purple Heart Corner. The town was extremely well defended, and we were going after a Messerschmitt factory. I was tucked in right close to the lead ship of my squadron, which had a lead pilot who was on his 25th mission. I saw this flight of two FW 190s coming in at 11 o'clock level, aiming right for our squadron. The fighters never veered, and the lead ship collided with the lead ship of my squadron and blew them out of the formation, and they exploded and his wing man scraped my top turret as he went across. We lost 12 out of our 18 airplanes in a flash. I had lost an engine...and got the plastic nose [of the ship] blown out.

Factories that made the Messerschmitt planes were very important targets. The Messerschmitt Bf 109 planes were some of the most powerful fighters. By destroying the factories that made these planes, the military could weaken Germany's abil-

The FW 190, shown here, was widely used in World War II.

FAST FACT

A FOCKE-WULF 190 (ALSO CALLED A FW 190) IS A SINGLE-SEATER GERMAN FIGHTER AIRCRAFT THAT WAS WIDELY USED IN WORLD WAR II. IT WAS THE ONLY FIGHTER AIRCRAFT IN THE WAR WITH ELECTRICAL LANDING GEAR AND FLAPS.

ity to defend its airspace. However, the Germans knew how important these factories were, so they protected them with heavy anti-aircraft guns and fighter aircraft often waited nearby to intercept incoming bombers.

John and his squadron made it home, but the Bloody 100 is known for its **catastrophic** number of losses. On August 17, 1943, 40 percent of their planes were lost over Regensburg. That same year on October 10, in a raid over Munster, only one plane returned. Within 109 days of combat, only 8 out of 35 crews came back alive. With how dangerous their missions were and how many losses they had, many crews referred to the unit as jinxed.

HOW YOU SEE HISTORY

1. Bomber crews knew the chances of surviving their missions were low. Why do you think so many soldiers continued flying despite the danger?
2. Many soldiers and airmen during World War II were only 18–21 years old. How might being so young affect the way they experienced combat?
3. How might repeated dangerous missions affect a pilot's confidence or how they feel mentally and emotionally over time?

CHAPTER TWO

A CLOSE CALL AT SEA

In 1943, as World War II was continuing, Allied leaders Franklin D. Roosevelt, Winston Churchill, and Joseph Stalin recognized the need to meet face-to-face to discuss how to finally bring an end to the war and defeat Germany and the rest of the Axis powers. This meeting, known as the Tehran Conference, determined how the Allies would defeat Germany and what the world may look like in the aftermath. In an interview with Bill, he discussed taking President Roosevelt to this meeting onboard the USS *Iowa* and a nearly dangerous accident that happened on this trip.

A TORPEDO MISTAKE

During World War II, leaders of the Allied powers had to make important decisions about how to defeat Germany and the other Axis powers. To do this, they sometimes traveled to meet and discuss military strategy. One of the most important meetings of the war was the Tehran Conference in 1943. President Franklin D. Roosevelt, Prime Minister Winston Churchill, and Soviet leader Joseph Stalin met between November 28 through December 1, 1943, to coordinate a final strategy

Scan this QR code to watch Bill discuss taking President Roosevelt to North Africa via the USS *Iowa* when it almost sunk from a torpedo.

Joseph Stalin, Franklin D. Roosevelt, and Winston Churchill are shown here during the Tehran Conference.

against Nazi Germany. This conference would shape the final years of World War II.

However, getting to these meetings could be incredibly dangerous. Enemy submarines and aircraft could threaten ships traveling across the ocean. Sometimes these threats were even accidental, which happened when Roosevelt was traveling on the USS *Iowa* for the Tehran

FAST FACT

DESTROYERS WERE SMALLER SHIPS DESIGNED TO PROTECT LARGER SHIPS FROM SUBMARINES AND OTHER ENEMY SHIPS. DURING TRAINING EXERCISES, DESTROYERS SOMETIMES PRACTICED FIRING TORPEDOES TO ENSURE CREWS WERE READY FOR COMBAT.

Conference. In his interview, Bill described the moment a torpedo almost hit the ship:

> *Churchill and Stalin were having a meeting at the Tehran conference in Iran, and Roosevelt was on the first leg of his journey to Tehran. Instead of flying, he wanted to make the first leg about USS* Iowa...

The USS *Iowa* was one of the newest and most powerful ships, designed to protect aircraft carriers and deliver powerful gunfire during battles. It had massive guns on board as well as thick armor, making it able to withstand tough combat. Even though it was built to withstand intense fighting, it still traveled along with several escort ships, especially since the president was on board. One of the escort ships on this trip to the conference was a destroyer called the USS *Willie D. Porter.*

The captain of the USS *Iowa* wanted to show how the ship was always ready for combat and placed crew members at their gun positions while the escort ships did similar drills. However, the *Willie D. Porter* accidentally fired a torpedo. Bill described the moment in his interview:

> *We had on our starboard side...the destroyer,* Willie D. Porter. *The captain of our ship wanted to show off and wanted to have all the men at their gun post, and so did* Willie D. Porter, *the destroyer.* Willie D. Porter *had their torpedo tube trained on us just like they were in combat. And they accidentally tripped that torpedo tube...Our code name was Lion, so they yelled "Lion, Lion, Lion, torpedo to starboard. This is no drill." I was a young ensign, I was 21 years old and I was on the main deck and the guns were up above me. [They] all started firing at that torpedo wake. I was down on the main deck and I thought, "I am too young to die right now." So it scared me. If they hit the torpedo or [it] made a*

FAST FACT

THE USS *IOWA* WAS ONE OF THE FASTEST BATTLESHIPS EVER BUILT. IT COULD TRAVEL UP TO 38 MPH (61 MPH), WHICH ALLOWED IT TO PROVIDE RAPID GUNFIRE SUPPORT DURING WORLD WAR II.

The USS *Iowa* was one of the fastest battleships used in World War II.

hard right turn, the torpedo went by us.

FAST FACT

TORPEDOES ARE SELF-PROPELLED WEAPONS USED UNDERWATER AND DESIGNED TO EXPLODE WHEN THEY HIT A SHIP. TORPEDOES WERE WIDELY USED IN WORLD WAR II.

If the torpedo had hit the battleship, it could have had catastrophic results: destroying the battleship, killing those on board, and potentially killing the president. Because of this incident, the *Willie D. Porter* and the crew onboard were all court-martialed to Bermuda. A court-martial is like a criminal trial but specifically for members of the military. Those who conduct the hearing are military officers, and penalties can include imprisonment, dishonorable discharge from the military, or reduction in military rank.

The officers who tried the *Willie D. Porter* crew found that they weren't trying to sabotage the mission or harm the president, and the USS *Iowa* crew got the president to the Tehran Conference safely.

THE TEHRAN CONFERENCE

At the Tehran Conference in late 1943, Roosevelt, Stalin, and Churchill coordinated their next steps in the war. One of the

PRESIDENT ROOSEVELT AND POLIO

Franklin D. Roosevelt was the 32nd president of the United States. One of the most notable things about Roosevelt is he had polio, which he was diagnosed with in 1921 when he was 39 years old. Polio is a very contagious disease that spreads through water or food. Many cases of polio are **asymptomatic**, but for about 1 in 200 people, it causes irreversible **paralysis** or death. This is because along with causing symptoms such as fever, sore throat, headache, and tiredness, the disease also destroys nerve cells that control muscles.

In the 1950s, a polio vaccine was widely administered, which led cases to drop drastically. However, polio is still a concern today in areas where not many people received the vaccine.

Roosevelt went to great lengths to hide the fact that he had polio because he didn't want the public to think he was weak or unable to lead the country. During this time in history, having a physical disability

Franklin D. Roosevelt had an agreement with the press to show him from the waist up, often sitting.

most important outcomes of the meeting was the agreement to launch a major invasion of Western Europe. This plan eventually became D-Day in 1944, when Allied forces landed in Nazi-occupied France. The leaders also decided that the Soviet

was connected with also having mental weakness. Roosevelt didn't want people to **pity** him, and he thought voters wouldn't trust someone with a physical disability to lead the country during the Great Depression and World War II.

To show that he was strong and active, he would hold onto his aides while walking or onto podiums while standing. Ramps were built at public venues so he wasn't shown being carried. He also used steel leg braces that were painted black to match his shoes and pants. He rarely was seen in his wheelchair in public, and he worked with the press to ensure they didn't photograph him in the wheelchair. Because of this, pictures show him from the waist up or sitting in cars.

The statue of Roosevelt in a wheelchair wasn't added to his memorial until 2001, after his grandchildren pushed for it.

Today, disability **advocates** have pushed for Roosevelt's full history to be acknowledged, which includes his disability. The Roosevelt memorial in Washington, DC, didn't have a statue of Roosevelt in a wheelchair when it was first dedicated in 1997. Sixteen of Roosevelt's grandchildren pushed for a statue to be added of him in his wheelchair, and the new statue was added in January of 2001.

Union would continue its offensive against Germany from the east at the same time, putting pressure on German forces from two directions. Opening this second front helped divide German forces and sped up the defeat of Germany.

At the conference, the leaders also discussed how they would cooperate for the rest of the war and began considering what Europe might look like afterward. Even though they had different goals and political systems, they recognized that working together was essential to ending the war.

The decisions made at the Tehran Conference determined how the rest of World War II would play out, showing how important cooperation and strategy was in addition to the battles themselves.

HOW YOU SEE HISTORY

1. Why was it important for leaders like Roosevelt, Churchill, and Stalin to meet in person during World War II?
2. How could the outcome of World War II have been different if Allied leaders had not worked together closely?
3. Why do you think the Navy investigated the *Willie D. Porter* crew even though the torpedo launch was accidental?

CHAPTER THREE

HOLDING THE LINE IN EUROPE

Some of the most dangerous missions in the war were carried out by Airborne units, whose soldiers were dropped behind enemy lines to capture key locations. The 82nd Airborne division was one of these units that had important roles in the final key battles of the war, leading the Allies to victory. In an interview with Ward, he discussed being a part of the 82nd Airborne unit, facing intense battles and long periods without supplies.

GENERAL PATTON'S ARMY

When Ward arrived in Europe, he first landed in Liverpool, England, which was a major port city that was a key base for Allied troops. The 325th gliders rode in engine-less aircraft that were towed by planes and released near battlefields. The gliders landed quickly in fields or open areas, which allowed soldiers to arrive with heavier weapons. In Ward's interview, he described the company he was assigned to and his first mission:

> *When we got to Liverpool, I was told that I had been assigned to the 82nd Airborne Division. And then when I got the location of the division, that's when I was told that I had been assigned to the 325th Glider*

Scan this QR code to watch Ward talk about the battles he was in and the thoughts going through his mind while fighting.

Members of the 325th Glider Regiment are shown here.

> FAST FACT
>
> THE 82ND AIRBORNE WAS ONE OF THE MOST FAMOUS AIRBORNE UNITS IN MILITARY HISTORY. THEY WERE WELL KNOWN FOR RAPIDLY DEPLOYING SOLDIERS AND PLAYED IMPORTANT ROLES IN SEVERAL BATTLES, INCLUDING NORMANDY AND THE BATTLE OF THE BULGE. THE UNIT WAS ABLE TO BE SENT ANYWHERE IN THE WORLD WITHIN 18 HOURS.

Regiment Company C... When I joined the division, I was with them probably a couple months, and we were assigned our first mission. We got to the airport and onboard the gliders, and we were told the mission was canceled, that George Patton's army had already overrun our drop zone.

General George S. Patton is one of the most famous American commanders of World War II. He was known for his aggressive leadership and fast-paced tactics, capturing more than 80,000 square miles (207,199 sq km) within just nine months after D-Day. In World War I, he was the first officer to be

George S. Patton, shown here, was one of the most aggressive generals of World War II.

assigned to a tank corp. In World War II, he continued being a master of tank warfare, using his aggressive tactics and speed to outflank the German forces, sometimes getting to and overrunning an area before the Allied forces even made it there. These rapid advances helped the Allies push deeper into Nazi-occupied territory.

BATTLE OF NIJMEGEN

Shortly after the canceled mission, Ward and his unit were given another dangerous mission in the Netherlands:

Patton is shown here with his army.

Two weeks later, we were assigned to go into Nijmegen, Holland, to hold and retain the Nijmegen Bridge...There were a lot of ***casualties****. We were without change of clothes or cleaning or anything like that for three weeks until other ally troops could come and fight their way to us. And fortunately they did. And that's when we were relieved from that mission.*

The Battle of Nijmegen, also known as the Liberation of Nijmegen, was part of Operation Market Garden. The mission was an attempt to end World War II by the Allies pushing their way into Germany. This battle in September of 1944 was crucial to securing the road and rail bridges before the Germans could destroy them and to also ensure the Allies could advance into Germany. If the Allies controlled the bridges, it would be quicker for them to move troops and tanks into Germany.

The Nijmegen Bridge was especially important because it crossed the Waal River, which was one of the largest in the Netherlands. German forces fought hard to keep control of it, and holding the bridge meant constant danger. The soldiers defending it faced constant artillery fire and air raids. Ward's unit, the 82nd Airborne, was critical to gaining control of the bridge. On the last

The 82nd Airborne are shown landing during Operation Market Garden.

day of the battle, September 20, the unit conducted a daylight assault, crossing the river in fragile canvas boats. The unit was able to seize the north end of the bridge, but they suffered heavy casualties to do so.

> **FAST FACT**
>
> OPERATION MARKET GARDEN WAS THE LARGEST AIRBORNE OPERATION OF WORLD WAR II. THOUSANDS OF SOLDIERS WERE DROPPED INTO THE NETHERLANDS TO CAPTURE THE BRIDGES AND ROADS NEEDED TO ADVANCE INTO GERMANY.

While the bridge was successfully captured, the city of Arnhem was not. The Allies were unable to secure the bridge at Arnhem and they suffered significant casualties. Arnhem and Nijmegen became dangerous frontline cities for five months. Failure to capture the bridge and Arnhem became **symbols** of the operation's **shortcomings**, resulting in a strategic setback and several more months of fighting.

Nijmegen and the Nijmegen Bridge are shown here after being hit during the battle.

British tanks are shown here crossing the Nijmegen Bridge during its capture.

FIGHTING AGAINST BELIEFS LIKE HITLER'S

Like many other soldiers, Ward was only 19 years old during these intense battles. They grew up during hardships like the Great Depression (1929–1939), which was a severe economic downtown with high rates of unemployment and poverty, as well as World War I. Many of these young men had little experience outside of their hometowns before joining the military. But they still believed the war was necessary. In his interview, Ward shared what went through his mind during these battles:

> *The first thing, I did not want a man like Adolf Hitler taking over our country. I did not want to see my mother and father, any relatives I had, the people of our country, have to live under the rule of a person like Adolf Hitler...And of course, the other thing was to get through it alive.*

Like many soldiers, Ward understood how dangerous Adolf Hitler and the beliefs he had were. His extreme political **ideology** was called Nazism, which was a combination of a dictatorship, **nationalism**, and racism. One of Hitler's most dangerous beliefs was the idea of racial superiority. He believed that people of German or "Aryan" background were the strongest and most valuable in the world, and he blamed many of Germany's problems on people he considered inferior, especially Jewish people.

One of the things that Allied soldiers were fighting for in World War II was to make sure beliefs like Adolf Hitler's, shown here, didn't spread.

Under Hitler's rule, Germany became a totalitarian state, meaning the government controlled nearly every part of life. The government used **propaganda**, censorship, and secret police to silence anyone who disagreed with them. People who criticized

Prisoners are shown here at Buchenwald concentration camp. They had to endure hours of role calls such as this through conditions like starvation, exhaustion, illness, and injuries.

the government could be arrested, imprisoned, or killed. For soldiers like Ward, fighting in the war meant trying to stop a government built on hatred, violence, and control before it could spread farther.

BATTLE OF THE BULGE

In late 1944, the Allies believed the war in Europe might be over soon. The German army was pushed out of France and the Allies were moving into Germany. But German forces had more plans to try to turn the war around.

In December 1944, German forces launched a surprise attack through the Ardennes Forest, a heavily wooded area in Belgium and Luxembourg. Hitler hoped the attack would split up the Allied armies and allow Germany to capture Antwerp. If Germany could cut off the Allies' supplies and divide their forces, the Allies would possibly be forced into peace talks.

The attacks caught Allies off guard. German troops, supported by tanks and artillery, pushed into the Allied lines. On maps, the

The Nazis forced Jewish people, Roma people, and others into concentration camps and death camps such as Auschwitz-Birkenau, shown here.

German advance created a bulge shape, which is how the battle got its name: Battle of the Bulge. In an interview, Ward described being sent to the battle:

> *We were offline in a rest area for about two weeks, a week and a half, something like that. And that's when the Battle of the Bulge broke out. And we were told we had to go online immediately, that the 82nd was supposed to go to Bastogne and the 101st Airborne to the Southern part of the breakthrough. We got to Bastogne*

FAST FACT

DURING THE BATTLE OF THE BULGE, THE 82ND AIRBORNE HAD MORE THAN 2,700 BATTLE CASUALTIES AND 1,626 NON-BATTLE CASUALTIES SUCH AS **FROSTBITE** AND **TRENCH FOOT**.

THE HOLOCAUST

One of the most **infamous** events to happen during World War II was the Holocaust, which was carried out by dictator Adolf Hitler and Nazi Germany. Between 1941 and 1945, Hitler and the Nazis systematically killed about six million Jews and millions more Roma people, people with disabilities, political opponents, and more.

The Nazis forced Jews to wear the Yellow Star of David on their clothing to identify themselves as Jewish.

The Holocaust started with legal discrimination against Jews in 1933, which removed Jews of their citizenship, closed Jewish businesses, and legally defined the term "Jewish" as being based on ancestry and race instead of religious belief. Discrimination against Jews expanded in the late 1930s with the establishment of the ghettos, where Jews were forced to live, and Jews also had to always wear a yellow Star of David on their clothes to identify themselves as Jewish.

The ghettos centralized the Jewish people, making it easier for the Nazis to load them onto crowded cattle cars and to concentration and death camps like Auschwitz-Birkenau, Treblinka, Belzec, Sobibor, and Majdanek.

before the 101st went through there. So they changed our mission and we were sent to the Southern end of the breakthrough.

The town of Bastogne, Belgium, became one of the most important locations in the battle. Several major roads passed through the town, making it a key transportation center. Whoever controlled Bastogne could easily move troops and supplies across the region.

Upon arriving to these camps, Jews were separated from their families into lines depending on if they could work. Those who couldn't work, such as children and the elderly, were immediately sent to the gas chambers, where pellets of poisonous Zyklon B gas were dropped into the enclosed rooms, killing those inside within minutes.

Those who weren't immediately sent to the gas chambers were starved and forced into difficult, brutal work. The workers faced starvation and extreme abuse, which made it even harder to survive in the camps. This slave labor was often fatal. In addition to these conditions, diseases such as typhus, dysentery, and malaria quickly spread due to the overcrowded conditions, total lack of hygiene, and starvation.

Jewish people were transported from the ghettos to concentration camps on train cars such as this. Many prisoners were crowded into the cars, not knowing what awaited them after they arrived at the camp.

As the German attack spread, Allied commanders rushed in airborne units like the 82nd Airborne division and 101st Airborne division to stop the advance. These units were **pivotal** to the battle and the Allies' success. The 82nd Airborne held the line, severely reducing and stopping powerful German forces without proper winter gear in the severe cold. The 101st Airborne held Bastogne while being surrounded by German forces for four days. The unit

A tank from the Battle of the Bulge is shown here in a World War II museum.

had to deal with severe cold during the winter, fighting in freezing and snowy conditions. They also had limited ammunition, food, and

Soldiers of the 101st Airborne are shown on the bottom right on the lookout for enemy tanks during the Battle of the Bulge.

American soldiers are shown here fighting during the Battle of the Bulge.

winter gear. Even through all this, they held Bastogne and significantly contributed to the Allies' victory. Their defense of Bastogne is considered one of the greatest and most heroic in US history.

HOW YOU SEE HISTORY

1. Why is important to study and continue to remember events like the Holocaust today?
2. Why was it important to take control of bridges and key cities during the war?
3. How might living conditions during the war affect soldiers' physical and mental health?

CHAPTER FOUR

PRISONERS OF WAR

World War II affected millions of people around the world. Soldiers who went off to fight sometimes disappeared in battle, leaving their families unsure if they were okay. Others were captured by enemy forces and became prisoners of war, or POWs. During the Battle of the Bulge in the winter of 1944–1945, thousands of American soldiers were captured by German forces. Some of them spent months in prison camps before the war ended. In an interview, one of these family members described what it was like when his brother was captured during the Battle of the Bulge.

LIFE AS A PRISONER OF WAR

The Battle of the Bulge was the largest battle fought by American forces during World War II and it was one of the last major German offensives of the war. After the Germans' defeat, they didn't have the strength to launch another attack. During the battle, more than 23,000 American soldiers were taken as POWs. In an interview, one man described his brother being taken as a POW:

My brother, oldest brother George was first missing and then a prisoner of war...He had gone to Texas A&M and they pulled him out and they had to go on in the service. He

Scan this QR code to watch a man discuss what his brother's experience was like as a prisoner of war.

These American soldiers became prisoners of war during the Battle of the Bulge.

went through training and then they sent him over to Europe, and he was captured in the Battle of the Bulge...He survived that, thank goodness, and they had a lot of problems in terms of his feet and things like that were frozen. He died at 63 at a very young age, but he had heart troubles for many years.

FAST FACT

DURING WORLD WAR II, THE US USED THE SELECTIVE SERVICE, ALSO KNOWN AS THE DRAFT, TO HELP FILL THE NEED FOR SOLDIERS IN BATTLES. THE SYSTEM REQUIRED MEN BETWEEN 18 AND 45 YEARS OF AGE TO REGISTER FOR MILITARY SERVICE. BETWEEN 1940 AND 1946, ABOUT 10 MILLION AMERICAN MEN WERE DRAFTED INTO THE MILITARY.

A prisoner of war is someone who is captured during combat. They would stay in prison camps until the war ended. Conditions in these camps varied depending on where prisoners were held and which country controlled the camp. Some prisoners received food and shelter, while others faced hunger, freezing conditions, and illness.

FAST FACT

APPROXIMATELY 23,000 AMERICAN SOLDIERS WENT MISSING OR WERE CAPTURED AS PRISONERS OF WAR DURING THE BATTLE OF THE BULGE. ABOUT 749 OF THESE PRISONERS OF WAR WERE MURDERED, WITH A LARGE NUMBER OF DEATHS HAPPENING DURING THE MALMEDY MASSACRE.

Germany had about 100 prison camps run by the Luftwaffe or Wehrmacht. Air force personnel were held in Stalag Lufts, which were the Luftwaffe camps, while ground forces were in Stalags. Prisoners were often crowded in wooden barracks, which were surrounded by barbed wire and guard towers. Food was limited and prisoners lost a lot of weight while in **captivity**.

During the winter, conditions were especially difficult because prisoners didn't have proper winter clothing or medical care. Because of this, illness, exhaustion, and frostbite were common. George's frozen feet were likely because of the harsh winter conditions during the Battle of the Bulge. Temperatures dropped below freezing, soldiers didn't have proper winter gear, and they spent long periods of time in the snow. Even after returning from the war, many former prisoners continued to suffer from health problems caused by the harsh conditions they were in.

THE MALMEDY MASSACRE

Being a prisoner of war was terrifying enough, but it was even more difficult and terrifying for soldiers who were Jewish and captured by Hitler's SS, or Schutzstaffel, which was a Nazi military organization. The SS was known for carrying out brutal actions during the war, including mass killings and war crimes. In his interview, George's brother described his fear being a Jewish POW:

> *He had become very close friends with a Catholic boy from Baton Rouge, Louisiana. Fellow's name was Billy Harriman...They're overseas and the battle starts and he's captured. [My brother] had on a Star of David and he was concerned because they were captured by the SS and they were shooting Jewish prisoners or that's what the rumor was. So he said to Billy, "what should I do?" and he said, "throw off your* ***mezuzah*** *and your dog tags*

GENEVA CONVENTION

The Geneva Convention, an international agreement started in 1949 in the aftermath of World War II, established rules for how prisoners of war should be treated. The rules require prisoners to be provided with food, shelter, and medical care. The agreement was designed to protect soldiers who weren't able to fight as well as civilians who may be caught in the middle of a conflict.

The first Geneva Convention was created in 1864 after businessman Henry Durant noticed wounded soldiers being neglected during the Battle of Solferino in 1859. He advocated for medical care to be provided to all wounded soldiers, no matter what their **nationality** was. His ideas led to international meetings where nations agreed on rules to protect wounded soldiers and prisoners of war.

After World War II, countries around the world met again in 1949 to expand and strengthen these rules. The updated Geneva Convention created clearer rules for how prisoners of war should be treated.

Under the updated rules, prisoners had to receive adequate food, shelter, clothing, and medical care. They can't be tortured or treated cruelly. Prisoners are also allowed to send letters to families and receive aid packages from organizations such as the Red Cross.

The convention rules also protect civilians living in war zones. They forbid attacks on hospitals, medical workers, and prisoners who are no longer fighting. Today, more than 196 countries recognize the Geneva Convention. Although violations still occur, the agreements are one of the most important efforts to protect lives during conflicts.

In 1949, more than 196 countries signed the Geneva Convention rules.

A memorial to people killed in the Malmedy Massacre is shown here at the site where they were murdered.

FAST FACT

MANY PRISONERS OF WAR RECEIVED CARE PACKAGES FROM THE RED CROSS. THE PACKAGES INCLUDED CANNED FOOD, CHOCOLATE, POWDERED MILK, AND SOMETIMES CIGARETTES TO HELP THEM GET THROUGH LONG MONTHS IN THE PRISON CAMPS.

and take mine," which he did. And when they came to George, he told he was Catholic and they went to Billy. And Billy had a really large Roman nose, and they asked Billy and Billy told them he was Catholic. They didn't believe him, but he was able to pull out his [hymn book] and quote from it.

Jewish soldiers faced particular danger if they were captured by Nazi forces. Because of the Nazis beliefs, Jewish prisoners were often separated from others and treated more harshly. Acts of friendship and bravery like Billy's helped some prisoners survive extremely dangerous situations.

An example of a mezuzah is shown here.

One of the most infamous war crimes of the Battle of the Bulge happened near Malmedy, Belgium, in December 1944. During the battle, members of an SS unit captured a group of American soldiers. Instead of sending them to a prison camp, the SS lined the prisoners

Hitlers SS carried out brutal actions during World War II.

up in eight rows and opened fire on the unarmed prisoners. One of the SS leaders then walked among the bodies and shot anyone who appeared to still be alive. More than 80 American prisoners were killed in what became known as the Malmedy Massacre. Just over 40 people survived the massacre by running into the woods or pretending to be dead.

News of the massacre spread quickly among Allied soldiers and made many afraid of being captured. After the war, several members of the SS unit responsible for the massacre were put on trial for war crimes.

HOW YOU SEE HISTORY

1. Why do you think international rules like the Geneva Conventions are important during wartime?
2. How might surviving harsh conditions as a prisoner affect a soldier for the rest of their life?
3. What challenges did prisoners of war face after being captured?

CHAPTER FIVE

THE END OF THE WAR AND ITS AFTERMATH

By 1945, World War II had raged for six years and affected nearly every part of the globe. Soldiers and civilians alike had endured unimaginable hardships, from intense battles to occupation and fear. In Europe, Allied forces were closing in on Germany, discovering concentration camps, and witnessing the devastation left behind by the Nazis. Meanwhile, the war in the Pacific continued, with U.S. forces fighting to defeat Japan. In an interview with Fiske, he described being a POW in Japan and finding out about the **devastating** atomic bombs on Hiroshima and Nagasaki from his captors.

WAR IN JAPAN

For much of the early years of World War II, the United States was not directly involved in the fighting. That changed on December 7, 1941, when Japan launched a surprise attack on the U.S. naval base at Pearl Harbor in Hawai'i. During the attack, hundreds of Japanese aircraft bombed American ships. Several battleships were damaged or destroyed and more than 2,400 Americans were killed. The attack shocked the country and quickly changed public opinion about the war.

Scan this QR code to watch Fiske discuss being a Japanese prisoner of war and how he escaped execution multiple times.

An exploding battleship in Pearl Harbor is shown here.

FAST FACT

NEARLY 85 MILLION PEOPLE DIED IN WORLD WAR II, WITH ABOUT 21–25 MILLION OF THOSE BEING MILITARY DEATHS. CIVILIAN DEATHS ARE EXCEPTIONALLY HIGH BECAUSE OF **GENOCIDE** IN THE HOLOCAUST AND THE BOMBINGS OF HIROSHIMA AND NAGASAKI.

The day after the attack, Roosevelt asked Congress to declare war on Japan, thus officially joining the Allied powers in World War II. In the years that followed, American forces fought Japan as well as Germany in naval battles and dangerous air missions. One of these missions involved Fiske, who was later captured as a POW. In an interview, he spoke about his experience:

My wing, the 313th, was designated to mine the Shimonoseki Straits, which is the main Japanese waterway...The Japanese had broken our code. They're shooting at us...heavy flames and smoke came into the forward cabin and I bailed out. I was over a big rice paddy, but a couple hundred civilian men, women, and children came in, proceeded to [try to] kill me. Japanese policemen saved me and one other prisoner. And it turned out it was my copilot Al Andrews. He and I were the only survivors... The other crew, all eleven of them were captured. We were special prisoners, not POWs. We were to be tried and executed for war crimes, killing innocent women and children, so we had no hope. And the prison got full. It had about 63 American prisoners in there. Toward the end of April, the guards came in the middle of the night and took 62 prisoners, Americans, out of this prison somewhere. They left two of us behind...the Japanese murdered all 62 of them.

The USS *Arizona* is one of the ships that sunk during attack on Pearl Harbor. It still sits in the ocean and can still be seen from the Pearl Harbor memorial that sits above the sunken ship.

THE MANHATTAN PROJECT

The Manhattan Project was a top-secret U.S. government program during World War II that developed the first atomic bombs. It began in 1939 after scientists warned that Nazi Germany might be working on a similar weapon. The project brought together some of the world's brightest minds in physics, chemistry, and engineering to create a bomb that could end the war.

The effort was enormous and highly secretive, involving more than 130,000 people across multiple sites in the United States and costing nearly $2 billion. In Los Alamos, New Mexico, scientists designed and built the bombs. In Oak Ridge, Tennessee, **uranium** was **enriched** for the bombs, and in Hanford, Washington, **plutonium** was produced for the bombs. General Leslie Groves oversaw the military operations, while physicist J. Robert Oppenheimer led the scientific team at Los Alamos.

The project produced two types of bombs: a uranium-based bomb and a plutonium-based bomb. These bombs were ultimately dropped on the Japanese cities of Hiroshima and Nagasaki in August 1945, causing massive destruction and contributing to Japan's surrender.

The Manhattan Project changed the course of history. It ended World War II in the Pacific but also introduced the nuclear age, sparking debates over ethics, war, and the dangers of atomic energy. It

Being captured by enemy forces in the Pacific War could be extremely dangerous. Unlike in Europe, where many prisoners were eventually sent to prison camps, some prisoners captured by Japanese forces faced harsh treatment, starvation, or execution. Fiske and the other prisoners believed they would soon be killed because the Japanese government accused them of committing war crimes because bombing raids had caused civilian deaths.

ATOMIC BOMBS

In August 1945, the United States used a powerful new weapon that had never been used in war before. American forces were moving closer to the Japanese mainland, but both the US and Japan knew that if they invaded Japan directly, it could lead to many casualties. To try to end the war quickly, the US decided to use a new, more powerful weapon called the atomic bomb.

left a lasting legacy in science, military strategy, and international politics, shaping the world's understanding of both technology and responsibility in warfare.

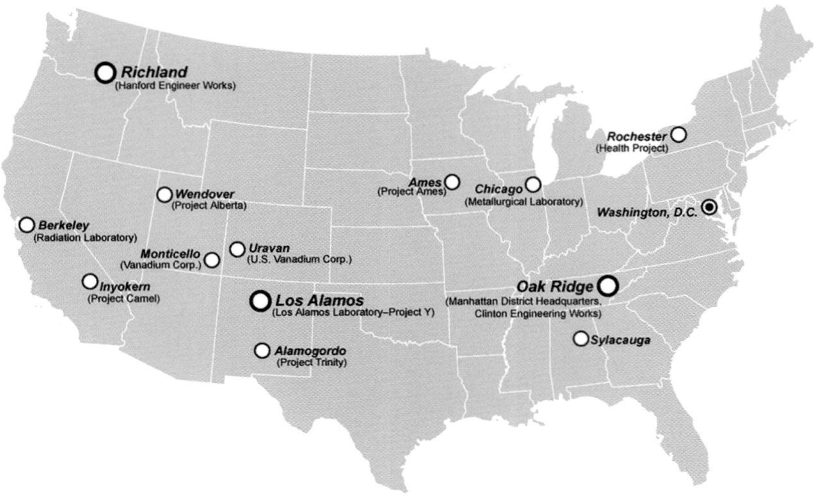

This map shows the location of sites involved in the Manhattan Project.

The bomb had been developed in a top-secret research program called the Manhattan Project.

In his interview, Fiske described hearing of this moment as a POW in Japan:

> *The Japanese came back after August the sixth and said, you people did a real bad thing. You dropped a bomb and you wiped out one of our cities...That was Hiroshima. [Then] Nagasaki got hit.*

FAST FACT

AN ATOMIC BOMB RELEASES ENERGY FROM SPLITTING ATOMS IN A PROCESS CALLED NUCLEAR FISSION. THE EXPLOSION PRODUCES EXTREME HEAT, A POWERFUL SHOCK WAVE, AND RADIATION. THE ATOMIC BOMBS USED IN WORLD WAR II WERE THE FIRST NUCLEAR WEAPONS USED IN WAR.

J. Robert Oppenheimer led the scientific team to develop the atomic bomb.

On August 6, the United States dropped an atomic bomb on the Japanese city of Hiroshima. The explosion destroyed much of the city and caused massive destruction within seconds. The explosion created a massive mushroom cloud made up of wind, steam, and radiation particles. It also created a 10,832 degree-Fahrenheit (6,000 degree Celsius) fireball. The mushroom-shaped cloud rose about 7–12 miles (11–19 km) in the sky, creating a thick, black smoke that stayed in the air for about 10 minutes. Many

The mushroom cloud after the Hiroshima bombing lasted about 10 minutes.

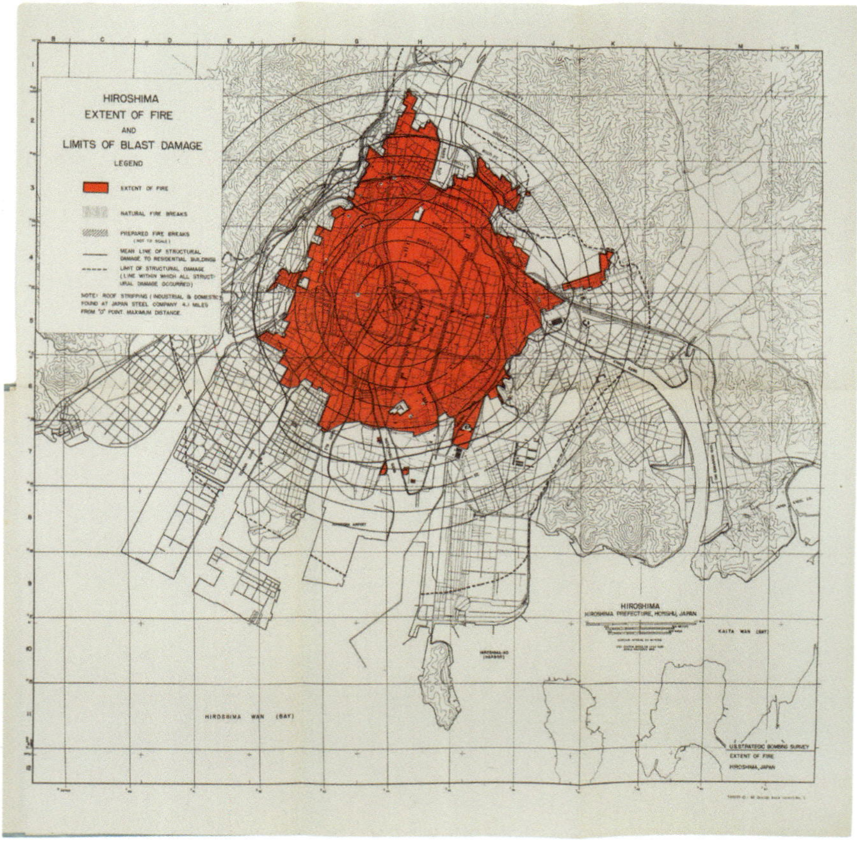

The extent of the Hiroshima bombing is shown on this map.

FAST FACT

SYMPTOMS OF HIGH-DOSE RADIATION SICKNESS AFTER HIROSHIMA AND NAGASAKI INCLUDED VOMITING, HAIR LOSS, BLEEDING, AND BLACK-AND-BLUE SKIN FROM SEVERE INTESTINAL DAMAGE. LONG-TERM EFFECTS FOR SURVIVORS INCLUDED INCREASED CANCER AND LEUKEMIA RATES AND REPRODUCTIVE ISSUES.

pictures were taken of this devastating cloud of smoke, which represented the total destruction of the city and the loss of 90,000–166,000 lives within four months.

Three days later on August 9, another atomic bomb was dropped on Nagasaki, resulting in more than 70,000 deaths. The bomb dropped on Nagasaki was more powerful because it was a plutonium bomb, but because of Nagasaki's hilly geography,

The ruins of Hiroshima after the bombing is shown here.

the blast was partly contained. Even though the bomb didn't have as intense an effect as it did on Hiroshima, the result was no less catastrophic. Both bombs caused significant loss of life and long-term effects such as radiation sickness.

END OF WORLD WAR II

By early 1945, World War II was beginning to turn strongly against Germany and Japan. In Europe, Allied forces were pushing toward Germany from the west while Soviet forces were advancing from the east. German cities had been heavily bombed, and the country was running out of soldiers, fuel, and supplies.

As Allied troops moved through Germany and nearby countries, they began discovering the horrors of the Nazi concentration camps where millions had been killed or were still imprisoned. Inside the camps, Allied soldiers found thousands of prisoners who had been starved, abused, and forced to work under brutal

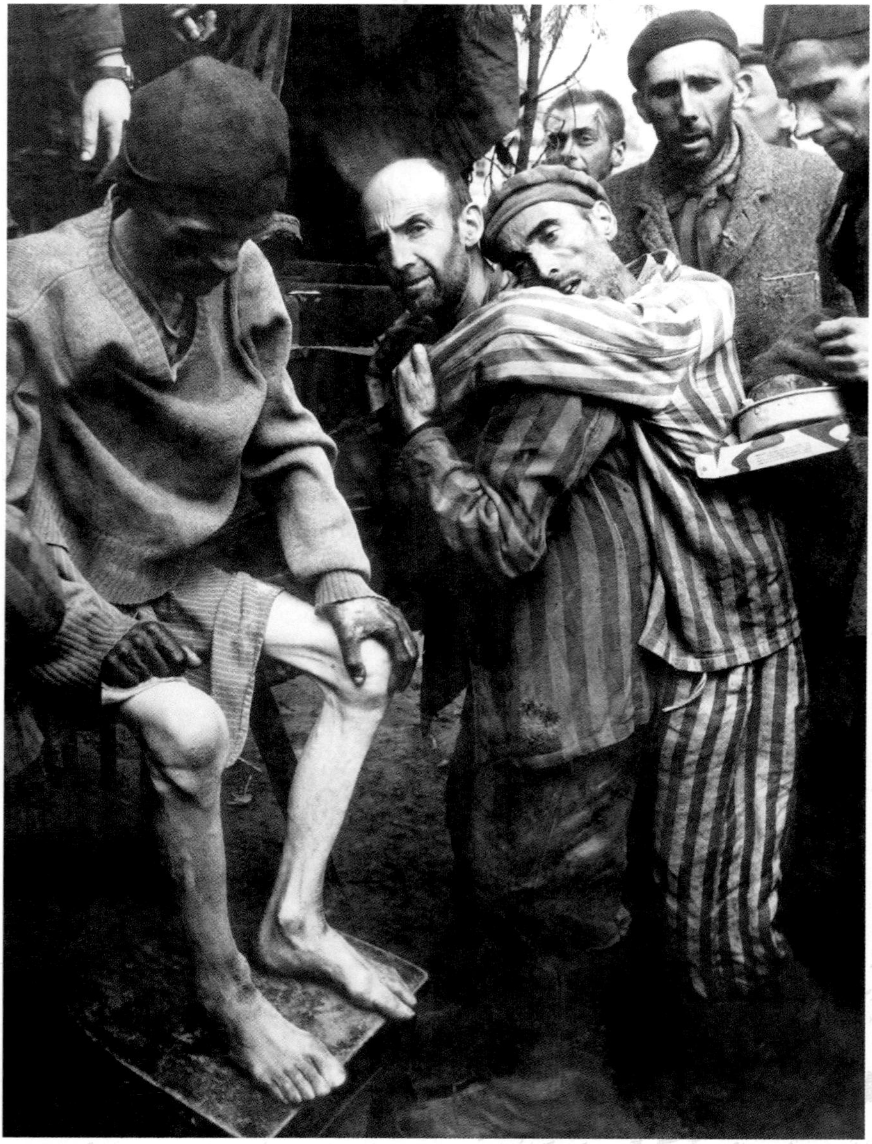

Allied soldiers liberating the concentration camps found the prisoners extremely thin and living in very poor conditions.

The National World War II Memorial was established in 2004.

Japanese leaders are shown here signing papers to surrender, officially ending World War II.

conditions. Many prisoners were extremely weak and **emaciated** after years of imprisonment. The liberation of these camps revealed the full scale of the Holocaust and shocked soldiers and civilians around the world.

Meanwhile, Germany's military situation continued to collapse. In April 1945, Allied forces surrounded the German capital of Berlin. Soon after this, Adolf Hitler took his own life in an underground bunker. Germany officially surrendered on May 8, 1945, which is remembered as Victory in Europe Day, or VE Day.

Although the war in Europe had ended, fighting in the Pacific between the United States and Japan continued for several more months. American forces continued their bombing campaigns against Japanese cities and military targets while preparing for a possible invasion of Japan. In August 1945, after the atomic bombings of Hiroshima and Nagasaki and the Soviet Union's entry into the war against Japan, Japanese leaders decided to surrender. On September 2, 1945, Japan formally surrendered, bringing an end to World War II.

HOW YOU SEE HISTORY

1. How did the development of the atomic bomb change warfare?
2. How did the liberation of concentration camps impact the world's understanding of human rights?
3. How might history have been different if nuclear weapons weren't developed?

TIMELINE

A CLOSE CALL AT SEA: TIMELINE OF WORLD WAR II

1943: The Tehran Conference is held to discuss how to finally bring an end to the war.

HOLDING THE LINE IN EUROPE: TIMELINE OF WORLD WAR II

1933: Hitler starts carrying out the Holocaust by removing Jewish citizenship in Germany, demanding they wear a yellow Star of David, and then by moving them to the ghettos.

1944: The Allied powers capture the Nijmegen Bridge, which was an important victory for ensuring the Allies could make their way into Germany.

1944: Germany starts the Battle of Bulge, one of the last major battles of the war.

PRISONERS OF WAR: TIMELINE OF WORLD WAR II

1944: SS officers murder more than 80 American prisoners of war in the Malmedy Massacre.

1949: The Geneva Convention rules are upgraded to protect prisoners of war.

THE END OF THE WAR AND ITS AFTERMATH: TIMELINE OF WORLD WAR II

December 7, 1941: The Japanese attack Pearl Harbor, Hawai'i, pulling the US into the war.

1939: The Manhattan Project begins.

May 8, 1945: Germany surrenders, which is remembered as Victory in Europe Day.

August 6, 1945: The US drops an atomic bomb on Hiroshima, killing nearly 166,000 people within four months.

August 9, 1945: The US drops an atomic bomb on Nagasaki, killing more than 70,000 people.

September 1945: Japan surrenders, bringing an end to World War II.

GLOSSARY

advocate: To support or defend a specific cause.
asymptomatic: Not showing signs of having a disease.
captivity: Being held as a prisoner or kept in a confined space.
casualties: People killed or injured in a war or accident.
catastrophic: An event causing severe hardship or destruction.
devastating: Causing severe damage or destruction.
emaciated: To be very thin and weak, especially from a lack of food or from illness.
enriched: Improving something through enhancement.
frostbite: A serious injury due to the skin and tissues freezing and damaging the skin.
genocide: The systematic destruction of a group of people based on their race, culture, or views.
ideology: A set of beliefs.
infamous: Being well-known for a bad quality.
mezuzah: A small case placed outside of the home that shows it's a Jewish person's home and they follow the Jewish faith.
nationalism: Strong devotion to one's nation and believing it's superior over others.
nationality: Belonging to a specific nation or country.
notorious: Being well-known for something negative.
paralysis: Unable to move.
pity: A feeling of sympathy or sadness for someone's suffering.
pivotal: Something that is very important to the development or success of something else.
plutonium: A highly radioactive and toxic material.
propaganda: Misleading information designed to influence people.
shortcomings: A flaw or weakness.
symbols: Something that stands for something else.
trench foot: A serious injury to the foot caused by exposure to cold and damp conditions, resulting in numbness, blisters, swelling, and tissue damage.
uranium: A radioactive material found in rocks, soil, and water.

FOR MORE INFORMATION

BOOKS

Ambrose, Stephen E. *The Good Fight: How World War II Was Won*. New York, NY: Atheneum Books for Young Readers, 2001.

Frank, Anne. *The Diary of a Young Girl*. New York, NY: Bantam Books, 1993.

Katz, Susan B. *The History of Pearl Harbor: A World War II Book for Kids*. Naperville, IL: Callisto Publishing, 2021.

Purnell, Sonia. *Agent Most Wanted: The Never-Before-Told Story of the Most Dangerous Spy of World War II*. New York, NY: Viking, 2022.

Thurlow, Setsuko. *Never Silent: A Hiroshima Survivor's Story*. Toronto, ON, Canada: Annick Press, 2025.

WEBSITES

Atomic Bombings of Hiroshima and Nagasaki
www.britannica.com/event/atomic-bombings-of-Hiroshima-and-Nagasaki
Learn more about the atomic bombs and Manhattan Project.

Pearl Harbor
www.nps.gov/perl/index.htm
Explore photos and more information on Pearl Harbor.

World War II
www.britannica.com/event/World-War-II
Read more about key battles in the war.

World War II
www.history.com/articles/world-war-ii-history
Explore photo galleries, timelines, and more.

World War II: In Depth
encyclopedia.ushmm.org/content/en/article/world-war-ii-in-depth
Learn more about the war and the Holocaust.

INDEX

PHOTO CREDITS

Cover, pp. 13, 27, 30, 44, 52 Everett Collection/Shutterstock.com; p. 7 USS California sinking-Pearl Harbor/Wikimedia Commons; p. 9 Legendary 100th BG, WWII pilot joins 100th ARW to remember 80th anniversary of 'Black Week' (8071155)/Wikimedia Commons; p. 10 Purple Heart Medal. Unknown recipient. (5388b05e-1dd8-b71b-0b3e-35d0c745d465)/Wikimedia Commons; p. 11 Pawel Bednarski 303/Shutterstock.com; p. 12 Wrecked hangar of the Messerschmitt factory at Augsburg, Germany, circa in June 1945 (342-C-K-3440)/ Wikimedia Commons; p. 14 OLEG PLESHKOV/Shutterstock.com; p. 17 Joseph Stalin, Franklin D Roosevelt and Winston Churchill, in Teheran, 1943, edit/Wikimedia Commons; p. 19 USS Iowa (BB-61), 1944/Wikimedia Commons; p. 20 courtesy of the Library of Congress; p. 21 Dennis MacDonald/Shutterstock.com; p. 24 TROOPS OF 325TH GLIDER INFANTRY MOVING THROUGH FOG TO A NEW POSITION/Wikimedia Commons; p. 25 George S. Patton 01/ Wikimedia Commons; p. 26 Patton in his jeep/Wikimedia Commons; p. 28 (top) Market-Garden - Nijmegen and the bridge/Wikimedia Commons; p. 28 (bottom) Operation 'market Garden' (the Battle For Arnhem)- 17 - 25 September 1944 EA44531/Wikimedia Commons; p. 29 Andreas Wolochow/Shutterstock.com; p. 31 caminoel/Shutterstock. com; p. 32 meunierd/Shutterstock.com; p. 33 Rick Siu/Shutterstock. com p. 34 (top) M.J.J. de Vaan/Shutterstock.com; p. 34 (bottom) On guard for enemy tanks/Wikimedia Commons; p. 35 Co G 38IR 2ID 16 Dec 1944/Wikimedia Commons; pp. 37, 48 courtesy of the National Archives; p. 39 Geneva Conventions - signing in 1949/Wikimedia Commons; p. 40 Malmedy-massacre-memorial/Wikimedia Commons; p. 41 Oleksandr Berh/Shutterstock.com; p. 42 Andreas Wolochow/ Shutterstock.com; p. 45 Allison Tackette/Shutterstock.com; p. 47 Manhattan Project US Map/Wikimedia Commons; p. 49 Hiroshima-Nagasaki/Wikimedia Commons; p. 50 Atomic Bomb Damage on Hiroshima/Wikimedia Commons; p. 51 The Second World War 1939-45- Victory and Aftermath IND5196/Wikimedia Commons; p. 53 Orhan Cam/Shutterstock.com; p. 54 Mamoru Shigemitsu signs the Instrument of Surrender, officially ending the Second World War/ Wikimedia Commons.

ABOUT THE AUTHOR

NICOLE HORNING is a published author of several nonfiction books for children and teens. She has her Bachelor's degree in English and a Master's degree in education. She doesn't just write for a living; she also enjoys it as a hobby. Nicole loves to collect books and read anything that sounds interesting to her. She also loves learning new things, especially historical topics. She does her best work while listening to Taylor Swift and having one of her two cats in her lap—both things happen a lot.